The ABRAHAM LINCOLN
You Never Knew

BY JAMES LINCOLN COLLIER

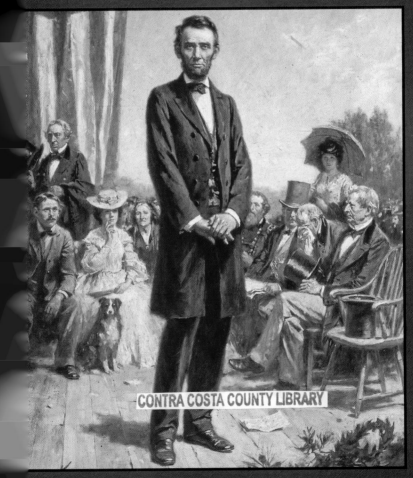

Children's Press®
A Division of Scholastic Inc.
New York Toronto London Auckland Sydney
Mexico City New Delhi Hong Kong
Danbury, Connecticut

Library of Congress Cataloging-in-Publication Data

Collier, James Lincoln, 1928-
  The Abraham Lincoln you never knew / by James Lincoln Collier;
illustrations by Greg Copeland.
       p. cm.
Summary: A biography of Abraham Lincoln that focuses on dispelling
common misconceptions and emphasizes how he lived his life with wisdom
and compassion.
Includes bibliographical references and index.
  ISBN 0-516-24348-9 (lib. bdg.)   0-516-25835-4 (pbk.)
  1. Lincoln, Abraham, 1809-1865—Juvenile literature. 2. Presidents—
United States—Biography—Juvenile literature. [1. Lincoln, Abraham,
1809-1865. 2. Presidents.] I. Copeland, Greg, ill. II. Title.
  E457.905.C635 2003
  973.7'092—dc21

                            2003005169

Illustrations by Greg Copeland
Book design by A. Natacha Pimentel C.

Photographs © 2003: Bridgeman Art Library International Ltd.,
London/New York: 1, 69 (Private Collection); Corbis Images: 31, 60, 63
(Bettman), 18, 23, 48, 51, 56, 57; Library of Congress: cover, 16; North
Wind Picture Archives: 4 (Nancy Carter), 7, 10, 13, 29, 33, 34, 37, 39, 46,
47, 54, 55, 58, 59, 62, 64, 65, 68, 71.

CONTENTS

IN THIS TEMPLE
AS IN THE HEARTS OF THE PEOPLE
FOR WHOM HE SAVED THE UNION
THE MEMORY OF ABRAHAM LINCOLN
IS ENSHRINED FOREVER

Chapter 1

A TOUGH UPBRINGING

NO AMERICAN PRESIDENT IS MORE idolized than Abraham Lincoln. We admire George Washington for his virtues and steadfast leadership during a great crisis; we honor Thomas Jefferson for his learning and brilliant mind; we respect Franklin D. Roosevelt for his courage and wisdom in guiding us through a time of great troubles. But we revere, indeed almost worship, Lincoln as we do no other of our great men and women.

Probably the best-known statue in the United States is the one of Lincoln at the Lincoln Memorial in Washington, D.C., an indication of how much Lincoln has been admired by generations of Americans.

His face is before us every day, the famous stern profile with the deep-set eyes, beaked nose, and short beard. That face is on our pennies, our five-dollar bills. It hangs from thousands of classroom walls. It has appeared on many different postage stamps. Carved in stone larger than life, it is there for all to see in one of America's most celebrated monuments, the Lincoln Memorial in Washington, D.C.

The Abraham Lincoln story is one of the first things we learn in school. We know that he was born in a log cabin and that he studied books by firelight because his family was too poor to afford lamps. We know that he "split rails" for fences, although few of us today could say what that meant. We know that he was kindly and wise, and that he freed the slaves. And finally, we know that he was assassinated by a crazed actor out to avenge the defeat of the South in the Civil War.

But Abraham Lincoln was not simply a man of godlike wisdom and compassion. He had his weaknesses, as he himself was well aware. He was not a god, but a human being. What was he really like?

Lincoln liked to say that he came from a poor and low-born family. That is not quite true. He was descended from Samuel Lincoln, one of the early Puritans to come to Massachusetts from England. Samuel Lincoln became a successful businessman. Some of Samuel's children and grandchildren moved to Virginia where they became wealthy farmers and were even elected to government offices.

Then, around the time of the American Revolution, Lincoln's grandfather heard from his distant cousin, the famous Daniel Boone, about the wonderful rich lands in Kentucky. The area was still mostly forest filled with Indians, but a hardworking family could do well there, Boone said.

A typical log cabin of Lincoln's time. Such cabins usually had few windows and often a dirt floor. The cabin shown here is set in the Blue Ridge Mountains. In Kentucky the land was less mountainous.

Lincoln's grandfather moved his family to Kentucky. He had three sons, and within a few years the family owned over five thousand acres of the best land in Kentucky. (An acre is about the size of a Little League baseball field.)

One day when the grandfather and his three sons were working in a cornfield, Indians burst out of the surrounding forest and shot Lincoln's grandfather. One of the sons raced away for help. The youngest, eight-year-old Thomas, sat beside his father's body. The oldest son snatched up a gun and ran for a nearby log cabin. He peered through a crack between the logs and saw an Indian sneaking up on his little brother. Quickly he slipped the rifle barrel through the crack, aimed at a piece of jewelry on the Indian's chest, and shot him dead.

If that boy had missed his shot, America today might well be divided into two countries, one in the North, one in the South. For eight-year-old Thomas Lincoln grew up to be Abraham Lincoln's father.

However, life for Thomas Lincoln was now changed. While his father lived, Thomas had been the son of a relatively well-to-do farmer. With the father dead, under the law of the time, his oldest brother inherited all the family property. This brother, Abraham's uncle, went on to become quite wealthy, and was an important figure in Kentucky, known for his fine racehorses.

Thomas was left with nothing. As soon as he was old enough, he went to work doing hard labor. In time he saved enough money to buy a small farm. And in 1806 he married a woman named Nancy Hanks.

The Hanks were small farmers just scraping along. Most of them could not read or write. Nancy Hanks did not find being married to Thomas Lincoln much different from the life she had always known. And on February 12, 1809, in a one-room log cabin, she gave birth to Abraham Lincoln.

It is hard for us today to imagine how difficult life was for these farm families living on the edge of the wilderness. The whole family ate, slept, cooked, and enjoyed themselves when they could in one room. The floor was dirt. All the heat, even in the dead of winter, came from the fireplace. On cold nights everybody tried to sleep as close to the fire as they could. Light came from candles, which could not be wasted, so that usually the family arose at daylight and went to bed when it grew dark.

There was little leisure time for fun. The family had to grow nearly all its own food. Corn was a staple. For humans it was ground into flour, which could be made into cornbread and corn pudding. The cows, pigs, and chickens also ate corn. The cow gave milk, the chickens laid eggs, and the pigs were usually slaughtered in the fall to provide ham and bacon through the winter.

Frontier families like the Lincolns also hunted and fished for food. Deer were plentiful, but sometimes they made their dinner of squirrel stew. It took a lot of squirrels to make a stew for four or five hungry people.

As a result, everybody worked, even small children. In the summer the whole family would be in the fields from sunup to sundown, plowing and planting corn, a large vegetable garden, perhaps wheat or rye as well. In summer they would cut hay for the cows and horses to eat in the winter. Haying always had to be on a hot day, for it was important that the hay be dry when it was stored in the barn. In the fall there were the hogs to butcher and smoke or salt down, apples and pears to pick, if they had fruit trees.

An artist's impression of Lincoln as a youth chopping wood. Actually, while logs might be split with a maul and an ax, they were usually cut into pieces for firewood with a saw.

The work might slow in the winter when the harvest was in, but there were always the logs to be hauled over frozen fields to the cabin. A family like the Lincolns might, in the course of a winter, burn a pile of wood that would fill up a modern living room hallway to the ceiling. That wood of course was not cut by machines, but with handsaws and axes.

One important consequence of all this work was that there was little time for school. When he was small, Abraham Lincoln did go to a school for a few weeks here and there in the winters. He probably did not learn much more than the alphabet and perhaps to add and subtract a bit.

Then, when Abe was not yet ten, his mother, Nancy Hanks Lincoln, became very ill. At that time there were no medicines for many of the diseases we now cure easily. Nancy died of her sickness. It was a terribly sad time for the family. Abe's older sister Sarah, who was eleven, now had to take over all the cooking and house cleaning, while the others were working in the fields. Often Sarah got so tired and lonesome that she could do nothing but sit by the fire and cry. Abe and his cousin Dennis, who had come to live with the Lincolns, tried to cheer her up. Dennis said later, "Me 'n' Abe got 'er a baby coon an' a turtle, an' tried to get a fawn but we couldn't ketch any."

Abe himself was very sad. Some people believe that his compassion for people, and even animals, grew out of his grief at the loss of his mother. It is certainly true that Abe

Lincoln did not like to see anything suffer. He would shout at other children when they were cruel to animals. He did not like hunting, but left that to others. Once, when he was somewhat older, he was crossing a freezing river with a wagon. His little dog jumped from the wagon and began struggling in the icy water. Lincoln leaped out of the wagon and waded waist deep in the freezing current to rescue the dog. This compassion would be part of Lincoln's character throughout his life.

At that time it was very difficult for a single parent to raise a family. Between the heavy farm work and looking after the children there was too much for one person to do. Thomas Lincoln began looking around for a new wife. He knew a woman who had lost her husband. Her name was Sarah Bush Johnston, and she had three children of her own. Quickly Sarah and Thomas Lincoln married.

Sarah brought her children to the Lincoln cabin. She also brought possessions, including blankets, a table, chairs, knives, and forks. To the Lincoln children such things seemed like luxuries. Sarah began improving

Sarah Bush Lincoln, Abe's stepmother, was a warmhearted, capable woman who encouraged her stepson as he tried to improve himself by diligent reading.

life for the family. She got the males to repair the house and put down a regular wooden floor. Things began to get better. More important, she brought affection into the children's lives.

She came to love her stepson Abe as much as her own children. Many years later she said, "Abe never gave me a cross word . . . His mind and mine—what little I had—seemed to move together." And speaking of Abe and her own son she said, "Both were good boys, but I must say . . . that Abe was the best boy I ever saw."

Like Nancy Hanks, Sarah was illiterate—she could not read or write. But she realized that learning was important. Lincoln's father, Thomas, who could write little more than his name, also believed that Abe ought to have some schooling. So Abe, along with some of the other children, was sent off to various schools, usually for a period of a few weeks each winter when work at home was slow. That stopped when he was fifteen; at that age he was considered a grown-up. Taken together, Abraham Lincoln's schooling added up to about a year.

But by this time another part of Abe's nature was beginning to show through. That was *ambition*. As we have seen, some of his relatives had done well for themselves. To Abe, his father appeared to be a failure. This may not have been a fair judgment, but it is one many young people make about their parents. Abe was determined that he would rise in the world.

He knew that to be a success he would have to have some schooling, as true as it was then as it is today. Even in the rough world of the frontier, nobody could go into business or the professions without being able to read and write well, do mathematics, and much else. So Abe set about educating himself. Fortunately, his schooling, however brief, had taught him to read and write. On the frontier, books were scarce and expensive. Abe read whatever he could get his hands on: the Bible, of course, history, many of the plays of Shakespeare, books on geography and mathematics. Nor did he just read these books; he studied them, sometimes memorizing long passages that he thought were important. He would give himself hard mathematics problems to solve. His stepmother, Sarah, later said, "He must understand everything—even to the smallest thing—minutely and exactly." And once he got something, he "never lost that fact."

One of the stories always told about the young Lincoln was that in the evenings he would study by the light from the fireplace. There is no definite evidence for this, but it is probably true, because lighting was expensive and had to be conserved. However, there is good evidence that in order to save paper, he often wrote out his math problems on a wooden board; when the board was filled with writing, he would shave off the surface with his knife to get a clean writing space.

One of the great myths about Lincoln was that he studied by firelight at night. He probably did, although there is no evidence for it. But he was an avid reader and carried something with him to read wherever he went. He read in spare moments during work and whenever else he could.

These, then, are two key points about Abraham Lincoln's character: his compassion for other living things, and his relentless determination to improve himself. He *must* get ahead.

But get ahead at what? Did he already have in a corner of his mind the thought that he might someday become president? Many ambitious young people do, although they are not likely to tell anyone. We know that as a teenager he read a biography of George Washington that "stirred his imagination." And later on he thought about the difficulties Washington and the other Founding Fathers endured to create this nation. It seemed to him "that there must have been something more than common that those men struggled for." They were great men, and we can suppose that Lincoln had already decided that he wanted to be a great man, too.

Chapter 2

FINDING HIS WAY

BY THE TIME LINCOLN WAS A TEENAGER the family was living in Indiana. Lincoln wanted to start his own life. However, he could not legally leave home until he was twenty-one. Besides, he was very fond of his stepmother and did not want to hurt her feelings by going.

An artist's idea of Abe Lincoln cutting down a tree. The ax is incorrectly held, as anyone who has used one will know. After Lincoln became famous, and particularly after his death, many highly romanticized images of him were produced, testifying to the great admiration in which he was held.

He did not particularly care for his father. We are not entirely sure why. We know that he considered his father a failure, perhaps unfairly, but that does not seem a good enough explanation. The two never had a fight, an open break, but later in life Lincoln did not have much good to say about his father.

Abe Lincoln became twenty-one in 1830. By this time the family had moved to a new farm on the Sangamon River in Illinois. Lincoln could now leave; he would make his way in Illinois.

Before he left, however, he took on the task of splitting rails for fences for the new farm. Livestock, especially cows, had to be fenced in so they wouldn't wander into fields and destroy the crops. The rails for these fences were made by splitting long logs lengthwise into quarters or eighths, depending on the diameter of the log. The splitter drove a big steel wedge, about ten inches long, into the log at one end. This would start a crack running down the log. The splitter then put a second wedge into the crack a few feet farther along the log. When he drove it in, the crack would widen, releasing the first wedge. This wedge in turn would be placed in the crack farther along and be driven in. So it would go until the log was split down to the far end.

The halves were then usually split into quarters, and if necessary the quarters split again. Log splitting was very hard work, because the wedges were driven by a maul, or type of sledgehammer that might weigh eight or ten pounds, far more than a baseball bat or even an ax. Rail-splitting was not the most important work Lincoln did as a young man, nor what he did most of. But when he became a politician some of his supporters decided that "the Rail-Splitter" was a good nickname for Abe, because it showed that he was a man of the people, the same sort of person as most of the voters around Illinois. Even today he is known by that name.

At twenty-one, when he moved away from his family, Abraham Lincoln was six feet four inches tall, and extremely skinny. His body down to his hips was of average size; it was the length of his legs that made him so tall. When he sat he seemed no higher than other people, but his knees would be higher than his hips.

He was also very strong, as was anyone who had done hard farm work from childhood. Big and strong, he was not afraid of anybody. He did not like to fight, but when he had to he could take care of himself. On the frontier, where many people were rough and there was a good deal of drinking—Lincoln himself never drank alcohol—fights were frequent. Once, when he was giving a speech, he saw one of his supporters being beaten up by somebody. He leaped off the platform, picked up the attacker, and threw him onto the ground. Not many people cared to tangle with Abe Lincoln.

It is usually said that Lincoln was homely. He said so himself. We do not have any pictures of Abe as a boy—photography was not invented until he was an adult. But the early pictures show a young man who, while hardly pretty, had a rugged manliness to him. His eyes were deep set, his nose prominent, his chin solid.

The Abraham Lincoln we are familiar with wore a beard. In fact, he grew his beard shortly before he became president. For most of his life he was clean-shaven, as he appears in this photograph taken in the 1840s.

What the photographs cannot show is the twinkle that frequently appeared in his eyes, and the sense of fun he carried everywhere with him. Even as a young man he had a great knack for telling stories and jokes. We must realize that in those days there was little professional entertainment. Farm people in villages and towns like the one Lincoln lived in might occasionally see a play or a concert put on by a traveling group, but mostly people made their own entertainment. They got up foot races and wrestling matches or organized dances if they could find somebody who could play the fiddle, played cards, or sang.

But mostly what they did was sit around and tell stories—about the strange or funny things they'd seen while traveling, about the foolishness of people they knew, or "whoppers"—tall tales of outsized heroes and events. Anyone who knew a lot of stories and could tell them well was bound to be popular. Lincoln soon found that he was welcome everywhere, especially among the rough farmers and river men who lived in these frontier towns, many of whom could not read.

But telling stories did not pay the rent. For some years Abe Lincoln worked at whatever jobs he could find, trying to make a path for himself. He worked on riverboats.

He clerked in grocery stores and at one period even owned one. At another time he was a mailman, riding around his neighborhood to deliver letters. He learned surveying from a book and for awhile worked at measuring off plots of land for buyers and sellers. Inevitably, he split rails. When fighting broke out between Indians and white settlers in what is known as the Black Hawk War, Lincoln joined a hastily formed militia. In these voluntary military units the soldiers usually elected their own officers. The popular Lincoln was elected leader of his company. His outfit did no fighting, however, and was disbanded after a few weeks.

More important, in 1832, when he was still a very young man, some of his friends urged him to run for the state legislature. He may have had some idea of getting into politics already; in any case, it was a logical step for an ambitious young man.

In the election Lincoln lost. But his appetite for politics had been sharpened, and in 1834 he ran for the legislature again. Once, when he was campaigning in a farm area, he came across some men cutting wheat. They challenged him to join them, saying they would only support a man who could handle the "cradle" used to harvest wheat.

Lincoln responded, "Boys, if that is all, I'm sure of your votes." He had, of course, done all sorts of farm work and knew how to work a cradle. He led the men around the field. In this election, he won.

To prepare for his term in the legislature, he bought an expensive suit with borrowed money. More important, he began to study law. In those days it was not necessary to go to law school to become a lawyer. Many young men "read" law in some established law firm. That is, they learned by doing. They looked things up for the lawyers in the firm, wrote out standard form letters and contracts, read about old cases to see how they had been decided.

At this time Lincoln could not read law in an office, as he had his legislator's job to do. But as he so often did, he began to read books on the law. As ever, he studied hard and memorized parts he thought important. Doggedly he slogged ahead; by the time his term in the legislature was over he had impressed many of the other members with his understanding of the law. Indeed, many of them asked his help in drawing up new laws they wanted to pass.

Then, in 1835, Abraham Lincoln fell in love. The young woman was Ann Rutledge, the daughter of a local tavern keeper. She was pretty, plump, and "goodhearted," a neighbor remembered. She and Lincoln became engaged to marry. Only a few months later Ann became sick with a serious disease, probably typhoid fever, a major killer at that time. She died two weeks later. Lincoln was crushed, and fell into a deep sadness. It was awhile before he could force himself to get back to work. Many years later he told a friend, "I did honestly and truly love the girl and think often—often of her now."

By now he had decided that he would become a lawyer. He continued his studies and gradually gained the respect of more experienced lawyers. Finally one of them asked him to join his office in Springfield, by then the capital of Illinois. In 1837 he moved to Springfield and entered a law office.

As ever, Abe Lincoln was determined and hardworking. Once he was defending a man accused of murder. A witness to the murder testified that he had seen the murder by the light of a full moon shining above. Carefully Lincoln got the man to repeat the story several times. Then he produced an almanac which showed that by the time of the murder the moon had already set. Many lawyers would not have thought to check something like that. But Lincoln always thought long and hard about things, looking at them from all angles. Frequently he saw points that others missed. His reputation began to grow, and in time he had all the work he could handle.

It must be admitted that he was casual about keeping things in order. He often carried important papers in his famous "stovepipe hat," a type that was fashionable at the time. And in one corner of his office there was a bundle of papers with a note attached that said, "When you can't find it anywhere else, look in this." But despite his casual ways, his reputation as an honest and clever lawyer continued to grow.

Lincoln in his famous "stovepipe" hat, a type that was popular at the time. He did not actually grow a beard until much later.

Then, in 1839, a pretty young woman named Mary Todd came to visit a relative in Springfield. Mary had gone to the best private schools. According to one biographer of Lincoln, she had "beautiful fair skin, light chestnut hair, and remarkably vivid blue eyes." She could be witty and sarcastic. She became very popular in Springfield with the young men.

The awkward and self-educated Lincoln was not at first her favorite among her suitors. But his honesty and intelligence shone forth. They both liked poetry and had similar opinions on politics. Gradually they became close. However, the relationship was stormy. Once Lincoln decided to break up with Mary, but after he did, he could hardly sleep. Soon the break was repaired.

In 1842 Abe Lincoln and Mary Todd got married. They had four children (although only one lived to become an adult). Sometimes there were problems in the marriage: Mary often ran up bills she shouldn't have and was sometimes too proud of herself. Nonetheless, they deeply loved and supported each other.

Mary Todd Lincoln was good-looking and intelligent, but she liked to have her way about things, as the stubborn thrust of her jaw in this picture shows. This drawing was done in 1861, shortly after the Lincolns moved into the White House.

Even though his legal career was going well, Abraham Lincoln was now sure that he wanted to stay in politics. At that time there were two major political parties—the Democratic Party we still have today and the Whig Party. The differences between the two parties are too complicated to discuss in a short book.

Lincoln was a Whig. As a Whig he served in the Illinois state legislature from 1834 to 1841. He was a representative to the United States Congress in Washington, D.C., for one term, from 1847 to 1849.

A big part of Lincoln's success in politics depended on his great ability as a speech maker. In those days, when there was so little professional entertainment, people enjoyed listening to long speeches, even serious political ones. They would willingly sit—or stand—through a speech of two or three hours. In many ways Americans of that time knew more about politics than we do today. Most of us only glance at the headlines in the newspapers or watch a few minutes of quick "bytes" on the evening news. In those days people would learn from long speeches all the facts and arguments for or against this or that idea.

Abraham Lincoln was not a natural speech maker. His voice was somewhat high-pitched, and his gestures were choppy and awkward. However, he was always able to make himself heard over a large crowd (there were, of course, no public-address systems). He knew how to throw in good stories to make his points. His arguments were always carefully worked out. People frequently came away from his speeches convinced that he was right.

Nonetheless, despite his success, he now had a growing family. He decided to stay out of politics for awhile in order to earn money as a lawyer and provide for his wife and children.

During the 1850s Abraham Lincoln began to do quite well as a lawyer. He had this house built in Springfield for his family, which now included three children. The front section was built first; the other sections were added later.

Even so, politics drew him back. In 1855 he ran for the United States Senate, but lost. He went back to practicing law, but by this time, even though he had not held public office for six years, he had become very well known in Illinois.

But now the great events of the time began to overtake him. He once wrote a friend, "I claim not to have controlled events, but confess plainly that events have controlled me." There was a good deal of truth in this: one of the greatest events in American history was about to break over the nation, beyond the control of anybody.

Chapter 3

A NATION BEGINS TO SPLIT

THE NORTH AND THE SOUTH HAD always been rivals, going back to the days even before the Revolution. By 1850 the North had built up a large industrial base. Cities were growing rapidly around factories turning out large amounts of all sorts of new products, like machine-made cloth, machine-made nails, machine-made everything else. The cities were tied together by ever-growing railroad lines and telegraph cables. The North, too, had a large banking system and other financial institutions. And it had a large fleet of merchant vessels.

This engraving, probably taken from a magazine of the period, shows workers in a factory making gun cartridges. The original of the engraving was in black-and-white; the color was added later.

The South had, of course, some railroads, some factories, a few merchant ships. But they had far fewer of these things than the North had. The South depended upon agriculture for its income. Southerners grew huge amounts of cotton, tobacco, rice, sugar, and much else, which they sold to the North, to the West Indies, to Europe.

Making matters worse for the South was the fact that the North had more than twice as many people as the South. Over the years the South had become increasingly fearful that the North would overpower it in both government and business. Even by 1850 there were some Southerners who felt that the Southern states ought to *secede*, that is, break away from the United States and form their own country.

But the wedge that would split the nation was another commodity the South had in great abundance—black slaves. Curiously, probably the majority of Southerners owned no slaves at all. A tiny minority had great plantations, mainly growing cotton, worked by hundreds of slaves. A much larger minority owned a few slaves who worked their small farms. Even so, almost all Southerners believed that they had a right, almost a duty, to keep slavery going. True, there was a small minority who believed that slavery was not good for the South, and a much tinier number who opposed slavery as being un-Christian. But most Southerners by far believed that slavery was right and proper, whether they owned slaves themselves or not.

Slaves picking cotton in the South. Actually, their clothes would have been ragged and incomplete, and an overseer with a lash would have been riding a horse among them to keep them hard at work. Once again, the color was added to this picture later.

In the years before 1850, Northern states had generally outlawed slavery. Over that time opposition to slavery had been growing. However, in the North feelings about African Americans were mixed. Some believed that blacks were inferior by nature and had to be ruled by whites, whether they were slave or free. Others believed that while blacks might be inferior, slavery was cruel and wrong and shouldn't be allowed. A small handful believed that African Americans were just as competent as whites and should be allowed the same freedoms. But whatever Northern whites believed about blacks, the *abolitionist* movement in the North to *abolish*, or end, slavery, was growing. It was growing not only in the number of people who supported the abolition of slavery, but the strength of their determination to do something about it.

The battle broke out over the admission of new states to the Union, as the United States was frequently termed. In the West there was a huge body of land that belonged to the United States but had not yet been cut up into states. People were rapidly filling up this land. Sooner or later they would have to be made states. Naturally, Southerners wanted slavery to be allowed in new states; the Northerners wanted it not to be. Over time, various compromises were worked out, but again and again these compromises did not hold. By the 1850s there was actually warfare in places like Kansas and Missouri between those who favored and those who opposed slavery.

Abraham Lincoln was not, and never would be, a strong abolitionist. However, his father had opposed slavery, which he thought was un-Christian, and Lincoln himself said that "he ever was, on principle and in feeling, opposed to slavery."

Nonetheless, in his earlier years, he had not given the question much thought. Like many Americans, it seemed to him that there were too many differences between black and white people for them ever to live together in harmony.

But he was not prejudiced against African Americans either. Frederick Douglass, perhaps the greatest black leader of that time, said that Lincoln was entirely free of "the popular prejudice against the colored race." As Lincoln became increasingly well known in Illinois, he became more and more opposed to slavery.

This picture shows some of the cheerful twinkle that many people noted in Lincoln's face.

But there was something that mattered to Abraham Lincoln more than slavery. It is important for us to understand that even today, only a minority of nations are true democracies, where all adults can vote for their leaders. At the time the United States Constitution was written in 1787 there really was no such thing as a democracy in our modern sense. Many, if not most, people genuinely believed that ordinary people were not capable of choosing good leaders and making wise decisions about how a nation should be run.

When the United States was formed, people all over the world were watching to see if this great experiment in democracy would work. (We need to remember that at first even the United States was only partly a democracy. Women, Indians, African Americans, and people with little or no property could not vote. Only gradually did everybody get the vote.)

By 1850 it was clear that the American experiment had succeeded. It had shown that ordinary people could indeed make decisions about their country. Everywhere people in other lands looked toward America and began trying to throw off their kings and princes to form democratic nations. Most of these efforts failed; but some succeeded, and the United States remained the shining hope of the world.

Many Americans understood this, and they felt proud and determined that America should continue to be the hope of the world. Lincoln was one of these. He believed that above all, this experiment *must not fail.*

To him, therefore, it was more important to keep the Union together than it was to abolish slavery. Like many other Americans, he thought that if slavery could be kept to the states where it originally existed, and was not allowed to spread, it would in time wither away. His idea, then, was to keep slavery out of the new states as much as possible, without breaking up the Union. Compromises with the South would probably have to be made; but the Union must be preserved. This may sound unfair to the black slaves, but it was realistic. If the South formed its own nation, slavery might well never end there. Keeping the Union together was the best hope of ending it.

In 1850, as the slavery dispute was coming to a boil, Lincoln was still a Whig. The Whigs were not hard-set against slavery. The Democrats, who had a lot of support in the South, were even less so. In 1854 some people around the Northern states who were determined to end slavery decided to form a new party. They called it the Republican Party—the same Republican Party that exists today. Very quickly it gathered members and grew in importance. Lincoln was now one of the best-known politicians in Illinois. The Republicans wanted him to come in with them. Lincoln was not sure what to do. He opposed slavery, that was true; but he was afraid that if the new Republican Party was too fierce in its fight against slavery, it might drive the South out of the Union.

However, the Whig Party was growing stale and sick. Lincoln saw that there were many moderate people in the Republican Party who agreed with him, and soon he joined. Very quickly he became the most important leader of the Republicans in Illinois.

In 1858 the Republicans nominated Lincoln as candidate for the Senate from Illinois. Lincoln had been thinking about his acceptance speech for some time. It proved to be one of his best-known ones. In it he set forth his main ideas. First, he quoted a well-known line from the Bible: "A house divided against itself cannot stand." Then he went on to say, "I believe this government cannot endure, permanently half *slave* and half *free*. I do not expect the Union to be *dissolved*—I do not expect the house to *fall*—but I *do* expect it will cease to be divided. It will become *all* one thing or *all* the other."

Lincoln's opponent for the Senate was Stephen Douglas, a very popular and well-known senator. The two made a nice contrast: Lincoln was very tall, Douglas was short; Lincoln was a sloppy dresser whose ankles often stuck out of the bottoms of his trousers, while Douglas was always carefully dressed in the most fashionable style; Lincoln was an awkward speaker, while Douglas was smooth and practiced.

OLD ABE
VS.
LITTLE GIANT

43

During the campaign the two men held a series of debates that are among the most famous in American history. They touched on many subjects, but slavery was one of the main ones. Americans, not only in Illinois, but elsewhere, followed the debates, which were reported in the newspapers. Lincoln was now becoming known across the nation.

In the end, the Republicans gained more votes than the Democrats, but for technical reasons Douglas was sent to the Senate. Lincoln was disappointed, but he said that the debates "gave me a hearing on the great and durable question of the age [that is slavery], which I could have had in no other way; and though I now sink out of view, and shall be forgotten, I believe that I have made some marks which will tell for the cause of civil liberty long after I am gone." He turned back to his neglected law practice in order to earn some money.

Far from sinking out of sight and being forgotten, Lincoln was now better known than ever. His debates with Stephen Douglas had convinced many people that he might make an excellent president. However, he had a lot going against him. He had no experience as governor of a state or mayor of a city to prepare him for the presidency.

While very popular in Illinois and well known elsewhere, he did not have a lot of allies and supporters in important eastern states like New York and Pennsylvania. As he told one newspaper editor, "I do not think myself fit for the Presidency."

But as we have seen, Abraham Lincoln was an ambitious man. And when he was offered a chance to make an important speech at Cooper Union in New York, he leaped at it. It would gain him much national attention.

Lincoln wanted to make his opinions clear. He was a moderate. He hoped to see slavery ended, but he knew that was impossible without destroying the Union. His policy would be to limit slavery to the places where it was entrenched but to prevent it from spreading. He ended the speech by saying, "Let us have faith that right makes might, and in that faith, let us, to the end, dare to do our duty as we understand it." It was one of the great speeches in American history. When Lincoln finished, this sophisticated New York audience stood, cheered, waved their hats and their handkerchiefs. Four New York newspapers printed the whole speech the next day. Abraham Lincoln was now a political star.

There would be a presidential election in the fall of 1860. There were other strong candidates for the Republican nomination for president. But in the end Lincoln got it. His main opponent was once again Stephen Douglas, the candidate for the Democrats.

Lincoln being sworn in as president in 1861 in front of the still unfinished Capitol. Although his voice tended to be high, he was able to project it so a large crowd like this could hear.

Douglas was not in favor of slavery. He believed that it was up to the people of each state, especially the new ones coming in, to chose for themselves whether to allow slavery in their state or not. While some Southerners were now insisting that slavery ought to be made legal everywhere in the United

States, most of them would have settled for Douglas's plan.

Unfortunately for Douglas, the Southerners who wanted slavery made legal everywhere decided not to support him. They put up their own candidate instead. The Democratic vote was thus split, and Lincoln won. Honest Abe, the Rail-Splitter, was now president of the United States.

Chapter 4

THE TERRIBLE WAR BEGINS

The CIVIL WAR OF 1861 TO 1865 IS certainly the most dramatic, and one of the most important, events in American history. It was the most bloody, too: over 600,000 men were killed in it. It continues to fascinate people. Over 50,000 books have been written about it, as well as countless articles, poems, and stories.

This is one of the most famous pictures of Abraham Lincoln. It was taken by Mathew Brady, perhaps the best-known photographer of the time. Brady took many pictures of Civil War battlefields, which even today help to give us an idea of the horrors of that war.

The election of Lincoln and the Republicans to the presidency upset Southerners. Many of them believed that Lincoln was out to take their slaves from them, which was not true. They also believed that the North had grown too powerful and was planning on making the South its servant. These people felt that it was finally time for the South to split from the Union and form its own government.

Not all Southerners wanted to leave the Union. In fact, it is possible that the majority would have preferred to stay. Particularly in the mountainous border states like Kentucky and the western part of Virginia (now West Virginia) most families did not own slaves. Such people resented the wealthy plantation owners in the lowlands who generally ran things in the South. In the end these border states, like Maryland and Kentucky, remained loyal to the Union, although there was always a minority of people in them who favored the Southern side.

But in other states feelings against the North were running strong, especially in the Deep South. On December 20, 1860, only a few weeks after Lincoln had been elected, South Carolina seceded from the Union and set itself up as an independent country. Over the next few weeks Louisiana, Georgia, Florida, Alabama, Mississippi, and Texas also seceded. They formed a government for themselves and elected a Southerner named Jefferson Davis president. They called their new nation the Confederate States of America.

Jefferson Davis, president of the Confederate States of America, is today seen by many as a villain of American history. He was, however, an intelligent and honorable man. He tended to be unbending and sure of his opinions and would not always take advice.

In those days a new president did not take over until the next March. The old president, James Buchanan, was still in office. Buchanan did not know what to do. He was a Pennsylvanian who disliked slavery, but he had some sympathy for the Southern point of view. He kept looking for compromises, but the South was not ready to give up their new nation and come back into the Union. No compromise was likely to work.

Of course the federal government had a lot of property and installations of various kinds in the states that had seceded. There were post offices everywhere, customs offices to collect taxes, forts, army camps, government warehouses, navy ships and docks. The Southern government began to take these over. Northerners were outraged, but Buchanan refused to do anything about it.

In fact, a lot of miscalculations were being made. Southerners believed that Northerners were not as tough as they were and would not fight. If they did fight, so Southerners believed, any good Southern man could easily beat a dozen Northerners.

In their turn, Northerners believed that with their huge advantage in population, manufacturing, railroads, and much else, the South could not possibly win. The North produced 97 percent of the nation's guns and 96 percent of its railroad equipment. It also had many more raw materials like coal and iron. Surely, Northerners believed, the South must understand they could not win against this advantage.

Thus matters stood on March 4, 1860, when Abraham Lincoln was sworn in as president. As Lincoln had tried to make clear to everybody, his first concern was not to end slavery, but to hold the Union together. He believed that the Constitution did not permit states to secede. He would not admit that any state had seceded. They still belonged to the

Union in his view. Therefore, the federal government had a right and duty to collect taxes in the South, deliver the mail there, control forts and other governmental buildings there. But obviously the federal government could not do any of these things unless it sent in troops.

However, Lincoln did not want to start a war. In his inaugural address he said, "We are not enemies, but friends. We must not be enemies. Though passion may have strained, it must not break, our bonds of affection."

However, matters had gone too far to be remedied by a speech. Still, Lincoln waited, hoping that if he gave everybody a little time to cool down a compromise could be worked out.

The flash point turned out to be Fort Sumter, located on an island in the harbor of Charleston, South Carolina. That state wanted to take over the fort, as it had other military installations. It set up cannon batteries to threaten the fort. The commander of the fort, Major Robert Anderson, sent a message to Lincoln that he could not hold out for long unless he had more men, food, and supplies. Lincoln knew that he had to stand firm against the South Carolinians, but he still did not want to trigger the war. He announced to the South Carolinians that he was sending food, but no arms or additional men, to Fort Sumter. This way the federal government would still control the fort without threatening the South.

But the South was not interested in compromising. On April 12, 1861, at 4:30 in the morning, Southern cannons began to fire on Fort Sumter. Major Anderson held out for a day and then was forced to surrender. The great Civil War had begun. Up until now some of the more Northern of the Southern states had remained in the Union, hoping that a compromise could get reached. Now they grew fearful that the North did indeed intend to dominate the South. Arkansas, Tennessee, North Carolina, and Virginia seceded. In all, eleven states had now joined the Confederacy. Only the people of mountainous western Virginia held out. They soon formed the new state of West Virginia, which would be loyal to the Union through the war.

The Civil War began when South Carolina bombarded the federal government's Fort Sumter in Charleston Harbor. As this picture shows, civilians came out to watch the bombardment.

It quickly became clear to Lincoln and others that one key to winning was to cut off trade between the new Confederacy and nations elsewhere friendly to it, like England. The English bought huge amounts of Southern cotton for their textile factories. They paid the South a lot of money for this cotton, which could be used by the Confederacy to buy guns, bullets, and other supplies. The federal government began to blockade Southern ports with their own ships. At first the blockade did not work very well; many Southern ships slipped in and out. But in time the Northern blockade improved.

One of the keys to the Union victory in the Civil War was a blockade of Southern supply lines. Union cruisers patrolled the waters near Southern ports to halt Confederate ships. At first, small, fast Southern ships taking out cotton to sell to foreign nations in exchange for weapons generally evaded the blockade. But over time, the Union blockade grew more effective, and the Southern supply line was choked off. This picture shows a blockade-runner trying to slip past the Union cruiser in the background.

Shortages of almost everything, from bullets to bread, were ultimately important in the Northern triumph. Nonetheless, the North could not win until its troops actually fought their way into the South and controlled things there. This was a big advantage for the South. It did not have to defeat the North: it only had to keep from being defeated itself. If Southern soldiers could keep the Northerners out, in time the North would get tired of the bloodshed and work out a peace that would leave the Confederate States an independent nation.

And for some time things worked out as the Southerners hoped. The Civil War is not easy to discuss, for it was fought at many different places at different times. Fighting might be going on in Virginia, Tennessee, and other places at the same time.

The first major battle took place near the town of Manassas, Virginia, by a little creek called Bull Run. It is known by both names. Several railroad lines met at Manassas.

There were two Battles of Bull Run (known as the Battles of Manassas in the South). They were both disastrous for the North, but the first one was far worse. Union troops fled in disorder, making many Northerners wonder if they could win the war. Here, soldiers pick up the dead and wounded from the battlefield after the fighting was over at the First Bull Run.

The Southern general stationed his army there to defend the railroad junction. The Union troops attacked. (Note that Northern forces were called either Federal or Union troops.) At first they forced the Southerners back. Then the Southerners, under the famous General "Stonewall" Jackson, held. For a time of heavy fighting the battle was even. Two Union cannon batteries blasted away at the Confederate troops. Then the Union cannoneers saw some fresh troops in blue uniforms, the Union color, come out of some nearby woods. They seemed like reinforcements, but suddenly they began to shout the rebel yell—"Yip, yip, yip," and charged the Union cannoneers.

The Federal troops fell back. A retreat turned into a panic and soon the disorganized Federal army was swarming back into Washington, D.C. The North had suffered a devastating defeat.

Now everybody knew that the war would not be easily won by either side. The Southern forces were commanded

An artis's view of Union troops in retreat from Chickahominy, Virginia, in late June 1862.

by General Robert E. Lee, still a celebrated name in the South. The Union troops were commanded by General George McClellan. He was very good at training troops, but slow to use them. Lincoln once said, "If General McClellan does not want to use the army, perhaps I can borrow it."

McClellan always believed that the enemy was much stronger than it actually was. In time, Lincoln replaced him with General Ulysses S. Grant, who turned out to be much more eager to attack.

The Battle of Bull Run was not the end of Northern troubles. There were more defeats and only sluggish movement by Lincoln's generals, especially McClellan, to bring the fight to the South. One of Lincoln's biggest problems was keeping spirits up in the North. After the battle of Bull Run one important New York newspaper even urged the president to give up the fight.

General George McClellan was a handsome, autocratic man much admired by his troops. He was excellent at training an army, but very slow to go into battle and quick to retreat. Eventually Lincoln fired him.

But Lincoln was not a quitter. It never entered his mind to ask the South for peace. He continued to look for ways to encourage the North to keep on fighting. His goal for the war, as we have seen, had always been to preserve the Union, not to end slavery. But by 1862 more and more Northerners were growing convinced that slavery had to be ended. They read the lists of the dead in the newspapers. Many of them had had sons and husbands and brothers killed in the war. Others of them had seen friends come home with one hand, one eye, one leg. Surely all this bloodshed had to have some meaning, some great purpose. Growing numbers of people were insisting that slavery must end.

Lincoln, too, was beginning to believe this. He had always believed that slavery was wrong. Now he began quietly to think about ways to end it. After many discussions with his cabinet, he decided that he would put out a proclamation about slavery. His cabinet members, however, warned him that he would only look silly if he issued such a proclamation when the North appeared to be losing the war.

So Lincoln bided his time. What he got was another defeat, once again at Bull Run. Yet again Union troops panicked and fled back into Washington. Lincoln was aghast. Lee, assuming that it would be awhile before Union troops would be ready to fight, split his forces. This time McClellan showed some spunk. He quickly reorganized his army.

With better generalship, the North might have won the Second Battle of Bull Run. Two generals failed to bring up reinforcements when they might have turned the tide. This picture, drawn by an eyewitness, shows the two armies fighting in close combat.

He caught Lee near Antietam Creek in Maryland. Federal troops were terribly ashamed of themselves for having run now twice at Bull Run. They were determined never again to flee—they would die first. One historian has said that sometimes "a sort of fighting madness" takes over men in battle. "This frenzy seemed to have prevailed at Antietam on a greater scale than in any previous Civil War battle." One soldier who was in the battle said, "The men are loading and firing with demoniacal fury and shouting and laughing hysterically." Both sides were badly battered, but Lee got the worse of it, and retreated.

It was the victory that Lincoln needed, although looked at coldly, it is clear that had McClellan been more daring, he might have chased Lee into Virginia and perhaps captured his army, which would have ended the war. Lincoln was furious with McClellan for missing the chance. Nonetheless, with the victory, he sent the famous Emancipation Proclamation out to the newspapers, which freed all the slaves in the rebellious states.

President Abraham Lincoln visits McClellan and his staff at the time of Antietam. Note how tall Lincoln was compared to the officers around him.

Of course, until the North actually won the war, the slaves remained under the lash of their owners. But the Emancipation Proclamation made it clear that if and when the North won, slavery would be ended in the United States. The Civil War was now about preserving the Union *and* ending slavery.

But Lincoln's troubles were far from over. It seemed that wherever he turned people were squabbling or criticizing him for things that he could do nothing about. Some Northerners thought that the Emancipation Proclamation was going too far, some thought it hadn't gone far enough. Others, tired of the bloodshed, wanted to

A Northern general talks to African Americans in Louisiana, which the Union forces took in 1862. Louisiana had a larger number of freed blacks than other Southern states, a few of them fairly prosperous. This picture may include some of those freedmen, mingling with the blacks newly freed by the Union army.

organize a peace conference. His own cabinet members were always arguing about one thing or another. Indeed, one of them was actually complaining to some senators about Lincoln. It was one of Lincoln's great strengths that in the end he always managed to hold his cabinet together, and to keep the nation determined to carry the fight on to victory.

But that victory looked far off. In late 1862, after yet another Federal defeat at a place called Fredericksburg, Virginia, Lincoln said, "We are now on the brink of destruction. It appears to me that the Almighty is against us, and I can hardly see a ray of hope."

But these melancholy moods did not last. Soon he would be the dogged Lincoln of old, ready to carry the fight on forever if necessary. His wife said, "He was a terribly firm man when he set his foot down . . . No man nor woman could rule him after he had made up his mind."

Nonetheless, by the summer of 1863 things looked very bad. Out in the West, General Grant had been trying for months to take the city of Vicksburg. The city was an important port on the Mississippi River.

General Ulysses S. Grant, shown on horseback, was willing to fight when McClellan was not. Eventually Lincoln put Grant in charge of the Union armies, and it was Grant who brought victory to the Union.

The North had taken the city of New Orleans, Mississippi, at the mouth of the Mississippi. If it could take Vicksburg it could control the river, preventing the South from using it for transportation. But Vicksburg was holding firm.

Things looked even worse at the beginning of July, when General Lee had decided to carry the fight into Pennsylvania. He had some good reasons for doing this. The blockade of Southern ports was by now hurting the South. The Confederacy was short of almost everything. In prosperous Pennsylvania, Lee would find barns full of corn and hay, warehouses full of shoes and rifles, stores full of food. For another thing, a victory in Pennsylvania would be very discouraging to the North and might persuade many Northerners that it was time to quit. Finally, such a victory might encourage other nations, especially England, which wanted Southern cotton, to come in on the side of the South. So Lee swung north.

Opposing him was General George Gordon Meade, who had just taken over his command. On June 30, 1863, some Southern troops entered the little town of Gettysburg, important only because several roads met there. As it happened, some Union troops were already in the town. They fought bravely, but were outnumbered, and had to retreat. One of the most famous battles in American history had begun.

The Union army now gathered just outside of town on high ground called Cemetery Ridge. Below it was a lush valley with fields of wheat and a peach orchard. Beyond the valley was another high area, called Seminary Ridge. Here Lee's forces set themselves up.

General Lee was an aggressive fighter who liked to attack. Like many Southerners, he believed that his men were tougher and braver than Northern men. Had they not won twice at Bull Run, at Fredericksburg, and elsewhere? He sent his army charging across the little valley and up Cemetery Ridge towards a stone wall that ran along the top. At the last moment, one Federal officer noticed that a hill called Little Round Top at the end of the ridge had no defenders on it. If the Southerners took it, they would be able to fire right down the Northern line.

Hastily he sent some troops from Maine onto Little Round Top. The Southerners charged up the hill, shouting the rebel yell. The men from Maine held firm. They fired until their ammunition ran out. A third of their men were down. Their commander told them to fix bayonets, and they charged down the hill at the Southern troops. The Southerners, exhausted from a day's hard fighting, began to surrender. At nightfall Cemetery Ridge was still in Union hands.

One of the most famous events of the Civil War was when Confederate troops under General George Pickett charged Union forces entrenched at the top of Cemetery Ridge. Some of Pickett's men actually managed to reach the Union lines, but were quickly killed or captured. With the failure of Pickett's Charge, the Confederate forces retreated. The Union victory at Gettysburg was a turning point in the war.

The beautiful valley was now filled with the bodies of the dead and dying. But Lee would not quit. The next day he sent 15,000 men charging across the valley and up Cemetery Ridge. The men struggled on in a fierce hail of gunfire. The charge almost worked. One group of Southerners actually broke through the Union line briefly. Soon they were hurled back, and in the end of the brief battle the Southerners were retreating to their lines, leaving behind half of their soldiers dead or wounded.

Gettysburg was a great victory for the North. The next day, July 4, there came the news that Grant had taken Vicksburg. The Mississippi was now a Union river. Although the war would go on for almost two more years, it was now clear that the North would win.

As was customary, the Union dead at Gettysburg were buried on the battlefield. A new cemetery, carefully designed, was laid out. A dedication ceremony was planned. Lincoln did not usually go to such events, but he wanted to make the importance of the Battle of Gettysburg clear. On November 19, 1863, he joined the elaborate dedication ceremony and made what is undoubtedly the most famous speech in American history.

Abraham Lincoln's Gettysburg Address, made during dedication ceremonies of a cemetery for war dead at Gettysburg, is the most celebrated speech in American history. In it, Lincoln made it clear that the Civil War must end slavery as well as preserve the Union. This artist's idea of the event shows people weeping, which was probably not the case. There is no good photograph of the famous speech.

Abraham Lincoln's Gettysburg Address was very short, lasting not much more than two minutes. It has been much written about. In the speech Lincoln did not boast of the Northern triumph, nor insult the South in any way. Nor did he say anything directly about slavery. He made two key points. One was that the soldiers who were buried there had given their lives so that the "government of the people, by the people, for the people, shall not perish from the earth." They had died to keep the American experiment going. The second was that the nation had originally been "conceived in Liberty, and dedicated to the proposition that all men are created equal." The words liberty and equal referred to slavery. Lincoln was saying that with a Northern victory, slavery would be ended everywhere in the United States.

For two more years the war ground on. The end came in the spring of 1865. Grant was now in charge of the Federal army. He bottled up Lee's forces at Petersburg, Virginia, where there were major railroad junctions. Slowly he tightened the noose. Lee's supplies began to run out. He decided that his only chance was to break out of Petersburg, and take his army south to join there with other Southern troops. They might then be able to hold off Northern forces long enough to force a peace treaty.

At the beginning of April Lee slipped his troops out of Petersburg. But Grant was alert and got between Lee and the route south. Lee kept pushing west, trying to turn, but Grant was too strong for him. At a little place called Appomattox Court House, Grant caught Lee. Lee knew it was finished. He told an aide, "There is nothing left for me to do but go and see General Grant, and I would rather die a thousand deaths." On April 9, 1865, Lee surrendered. The dreadful war was at last over.

Many Northerners wanted to take direful revenge on the South, but Lincoln would have none of it. In his famous second inaugural address, he said that, "With malice towards none; with charity for all . . . let us strive on to finish the work we are in; to bind up the nation's wounds."

Lincoln's popularity in the North was immense. People had finally come to understand that he was a great president. He had, over immense difficulties, saved the nation and ended slavery. If he had remained president he would have certainly tried to work with the South to rebuild it after the horrors of four years of war.

This artist's version shows the surrender at Appomattox. Lee is signing the surrender paper, while Grant stands and watches. The terrible war was finally over.

But he did not remain president. Only five days after the Federal victory, a crazed actor named John Wilkes Booth, determined to avenge the South, slipped into a theater where Lincoln was watching a play and shot him in the back of his head. Lincoln was carried, still alive, but unconscious, to a nearby house. Through the night the president lingered. Early in the morning he died. Edwin Stanton, one of Lincoln's cabinet members, was standing at the foot of the bed. He put his hat on briefly, then took it off again in salute. "Now he belongs to the ages," he said.

What made Lincoln a great man? For one thing, there was his kindness. He hated to hurt anybody and was always doing small favors for people. He loved romping with his sons. Once, during a formal reception in the White House, his son Tad hitched his pet goat to a chair and drove into the reception, weaving in and out among the well-dressed guests. Everyone was astonished; Lincoln simply laughed.

Furthermore, he was not vengeful, not always trying to get even with people. After he discovered the cabinet member complaining about him behind his back, he did not fire him, but kept him in office to keep things running smoothly.

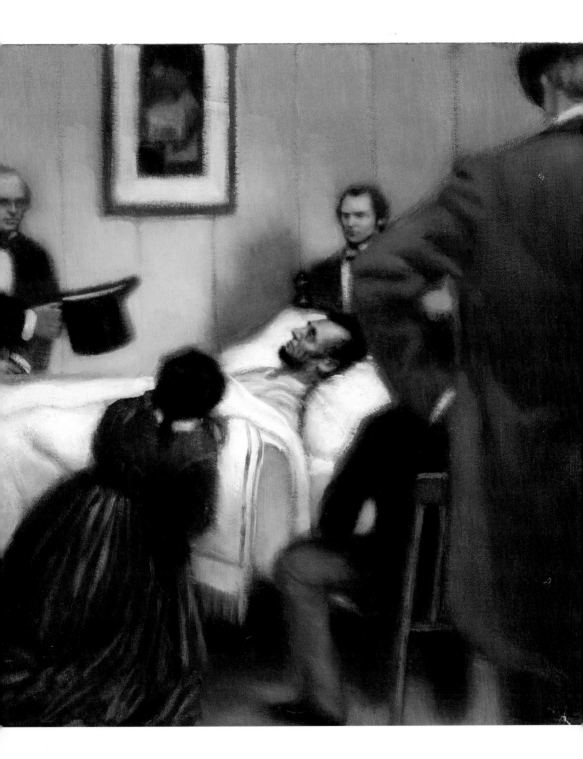

With this sort of personality, it is certainly true that he would have worked hard to see that African Americans gained true equality with whites. Without Lincoln, that would prove a long time coming.

For another thing, Lincoln believed that people must use their minds to control their *passions*. People must not act on their feelings, their first impulses, but must think things through to figure what was best to do. He always took time to come to decisions. For example, he did not rush to the defense of Fort Sumter, but he did not abandon the fort, either. He watched, waited, and thought, until he had looked at all the possibilities, and chose the one he thought had the best chance of working.

Finally, Abraham Lincoln had a very firm sense of right and wrong. Early in his career as a lawyer he became known as "Honest Abe," a man who could be trusted with your money, who would not lie. In one lecture he advised young lawyers, "Resolve to be honest at all events; and if, in your own judgment you cannot be an honest lawyer, resolve to be honest without being a lawyer. Choose some other occupation."

When it came to slavery he was under a lot of pressure to compromise. But in the end, after much thought, he concluded that slavery was simply wrong. Some Southerners argued that slavery was good for African Americans because it gave them security—they always knew that they would have food and a place to sleep. Lincoln answered that you never heard of a free person choosing to become a slave just to get food and a bed. Even the most foolish slave, he added, "does constantly *know* that he is wronged."

Lincoln's compassion was part of his thinking. When he took up a problem, he always thought about how this or that solution might affect other people. He was, it is true, slow to come to a decision. He should have fired General McClellan long before he did, for example. But once he had thought a thing through, and was sure he was right, he wouldn't budge. Once he asked the cabinet how they felt about a certain matter. The vote was nine nays, one aye. "The ayes have it," Lincoln said. He was certain he was right, because he had heard all the other possibilities, considered them, and knew there was only one choice.

Abraham Lincoln had, then, both wisdom and compassion. It is rare for any of us to have either quality. Lincoln had them both, and that is why we continue to admire him so much.

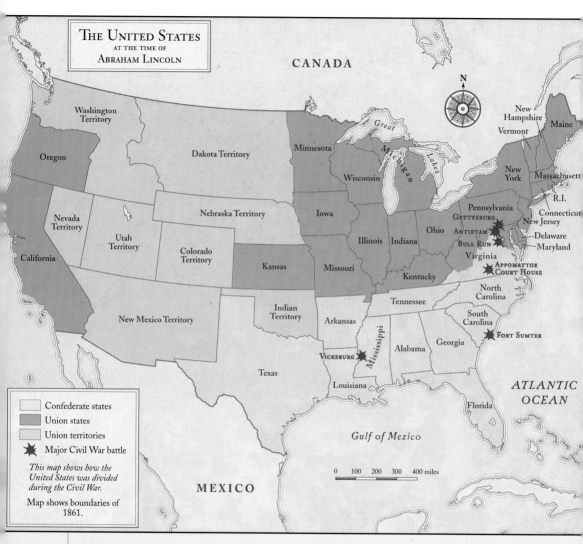

THE UNITED STATES
AT THE TIME OF
ABRAHAM LINCOLN

CANADA

N

Washington Territory

Oregon

Dakota Territory

Minnesota

Great

Michigan

Lakes

New Hampshire

Vermont

Maine

Nevada Territory

Utah Territory

Nebraska Territory

Wisconsin

Iowa

New York

Massachusett

R.I.

California

Colorado Territory

Kansas

Missouri

Illinois

Indiana

Ohio

Pennsylvania

GETTYSBURG

ANTIETAM

BULL RUN

Virginia

Connecticut

New Jersey

Delaware

Maryland

APPOMATTOX
COURT HOUSE

New Mexico Territory

Indian Territory

Arkansas

Tennessee

Kentucky

North Carolina

South Carolina

Georgia

FORT SUMTER

Texas

VICKSBURG

Mississippi

Louisiana

Alabama

Florida

ATLANTIC
OCEAN

Gulf of Mexico

MEXICO

Confederate states

Union states

Union territories

Major Civil War battle

This map shows how the United States was divided during the Civil War.

Map shows boundaries of 1861.

0   100   200   300   400 miles

As this map shows, the Civil War was a complicated story, fought over a large area. While the critically important Battle of Gettysburg was going on in Pennsylvania, another vitally important fight was occuring at Vicksburg, some twelve hundred miles away. The map shows only a few of the many battles fought, mainly in the Southern states, during the Civil War.

Author's Note on Sources

There is such a large amount of material on Abraham Lincoln and the Civil War that it is difficult to pick among them. An excellent recent biography is *Lincoln*, by David H. Donald. For younger students there is *Lincoln*, by Roger Bruns. For the Civil War, there is *Echoes of Glory*, by the editors of Time-Life Books, and *The Civil War: A House Divided*, by Zachary Kent.

Bruns, Roger. *Lincoln*. New York: Chelsea House Publishers, 1986. (young readers)

Donald, David Herbert. *Lincoln*. New York: Simon & Schuster, 1995.

Marrin, Albert. *Abraham Lincoln and the Civil War*. New York, Dutton, 1997.

INDEX

ABOUT THE AUTHOR

James Lincoln Collier has written many books, both fiction and nonfiction, for children and adults. His interests span history, biography, and historical fiction. He is an authority on the history of jazz and performs weekly on the trombone in New York City.

My Brother Sam Is Dead was named a Newbery Honor Book and a Jane Addams Honor Book and was a finalist for a National Book Award. *Jump Ship to Freedom* and *War Comes to Willy Freemen* were each named a notable Children's Trade Book in the Field of Social Studies by the National Council for Social Studies and the Children's Book Council. Collier received the Christopher Award for *Decision in Philadelphia: The Constitutional Convention of 1787*. He lives in Pawling, New York.